Lost Sheep

LOST
SHEEP

Foreword 2022

I am both Messianic Jewish and Christian. Some might say, how could this be?

It's very simple.

When Moses went and told the people all the LORD's words and laws, they responded with one voice, "Everything the LORD has said we will do."

- Exodus 24:3

This is the day known as Shavuot. Pentecost itself, is the anniversary of this day - the day we said, "I do." It's a wedding contract. These are vows that we cannot fulfill without our Lord and Savior Jesus. The Holy Spirit was an anniversary gift: His presence in us.

So, Moses went back and summoned the elders of the people and set before them all the words the LORD had commanded him to speak.

*The people all responded together,
"We will do everything the LORD has
said." So, Moses brought their
answer back to the LORD.*

- Exodus 19:7-8

    Jesus is the Groom, we (the children of Abraham - saved by His Blood) are the Bride. Like any other marriage, we are married by Grace. We commit to any marriage with the promise that we will both fulfill our vows.

    We cannot fulfill these vows without Jesus, nor should we try. He is the reason for the Vows, and only through the power of His Grace can we understand what the Vows (Commandments) mean.

    He shows us through our relationship with Him. Otherwise, it is just legalism.

Love fulfills the Law: our love for Jesus.

Let no debt remain outstanding, except the continuing debt to love another, for whoever loves others has fulfilled the law. The Commandments, "You shall not commit adultery," "You shall not murder," "You shall not steal," "You shall not covet," and whatever other command there may be, are summed up in this one command: "Love your neighbor as yourself." Love does no harm to a neighbor. Therefore, love is the fulfillment of the law."

- Romans 13:8-10

Grace picks us up and carries us when we fall short of the Law (The Torah or wedding contract). Jesus is the LIVING Word. God is a God of the living, not of the dead.

Paul never stopped confessing the wedding contract or his commitment to these vows.

I believe everything that is in accordance with the Law and that is written in the Prophets. - Acts 24:14

However, he was not foolish enough to believe that he could fulfill these vows without Jesus and the power of Grace.

Then Paul made his defense: "I have done nothing wrong against the Jewish Law or against the temple or against Caesar." -Acts 25:8

These statements went over the heads of the Jewish leaders.

I have NO problem believing in or following the Torah, as the Messianic Jewish confess. However, I am not foolish enough to believe I can fulfill these vows without Jesus. Let's not forget, He is the whole point of the Vows.

Some Christians insist we must throw out the wedding vows. While Messianic Jewish forget that we are saved by Grace.

It has been my experience that sometimes Messianics need more Jesus, and sometimes Christians need more Yeshua.

To enter the kingdom, we must be born again. So, my Messianic brethren: do not forget John Chapter 3. Grace gets you in the door (Romans 10:9), obedience - with the help of Jesus - keeps you in the blessing (1 John 2:30).

People still need to be saved by the Blood of Jesus. Messianics should never forget their Christian roots. Sure, the Catholic Church (or more specifically, The Roman Empire) has corrupted some things... but let's never forget the price that was paid (in full) for our salvation.

Your brother in Christ,

Frank DeF

Broken Road
Ministries

The Roman Empire corrupted worship of the Messiah. Because they were a polytheistic culture (worshipped many gods), they added pagan names, holidays, and other pagan elements to what the Apostles were doing. Paul had warned that this would eventually happen. Some believers jump ship to other religions which do not serve the God of Abraham, Isaac, and Jacob. The hurt of being lied to by the Catholic Church makes them vulnerable to paradigms which do not acknowledge that Yeshua died and rose again on the third day.

Broken Road Ministries acknowledges that yes, some things were changed. Yes, you did not get the whole truth about some things. But never doubt for one minute the sacrifice that Jesus made and how important it is for your salvation. We are fishers of men. As fishers of men, it is our responsibility to get this right, and to bring back to the sheepfold those brothers who have wandered.

The Messianic Movement is Christianity without the added paganism. But it also acknowledges where Christianity got it right and how important it is that we all stick together as brothers of the Way, the Truth, and the Life.

- Your Brother In Christ, Frank DeF

Sinners Prayer

You shall receive power when the Holy Spirit has come upon you; and you shall be witnesses to Me in Jerusalem, and in all Judea and Samaria, and to the end of the earth. -Acts 1:8 (NKJV)

How do we receive the Holy Spirit?

If ye then, being evil, know how to give good gifts unto your children: how much more shall your heavenly Father give the Holy Spirit to them that ask him? -Luke 11:13 (KJV)

I often say the following prayer, as an exercise in obedience. Every day we must come to the foot of the cross and negotiate the terms of a full surrender.

Adon Yeshua, my heart is restless, and I need you. I am filled with a deep sorrow for my sins. I ask for Your forgiveness. I believe You came and died for my sins, and that You rose again on the third day. By grace through faith, I receive You as my Adon and Savior and Master. Thank you Adon Yeshua for giving me the gift of eternal life. Thank you Adon Yeshua for the promise of an abundant life. Please continue to change me from the inside out. Amen.

Elohim will meet you where you're at, but He won't let you stay there forever.

And by this we know that we have come to know Him, if we keep His commandments. Whoever says, "I know Him" but does not keep His commandments is a liar, and the truth is not in him, but whoever keeps His word, in him truly the love of God is perfected. By this we may know that we are in him: whoever says he abides in Him ought to walk in the same way in which He walked. -1 John 2:3-6 (ESV)

You have to be in fellowship with Elohim if you want Him to answer your prayers. How do you get to know Elohim better? Read the bible. Yeshua is in the word in the flesh. Ask Him to speak to you through the word.

eternity

forgiveness
breaks the hold
where
the depth unolds
i begin
to understand eternity

faith
with an exclamation
the enemy of frustration
you O YHWH
live in the impossible

you raised me
from the dead
you are my breath
forever
instead of death

covenant of blood
with the Son
Yeshua
is the one
who saves
there is power
in the name

regeneration
despite temptation
there is now no
condemnation

mankind will
ascend time
The Holy Spirit
will lift
we are
the spiritual gifts

this endless
love pleasing
in his sight
walk as children
of light

the fire in the faithful

bringing purpose
to reality
to establish
forever
the whosoever

born of the Spirit
still higher gifts
to come
positive
imaginations
that bend
to the will of YHWH

the foundation
of my faith
to master
trust
belief
my passions
at peace

soldiers of love
who serve
the grace
we don't deserve

your precious love

sing her lullabies
the caress
of your angels
overwhelming
peace
and holy
whispers

she is
a morning star
the opening eyes
of faith

your unfailing love

prayer for the
protection of
Rachel

may Your Word
have
free course
in her life

reign of peace

Yeshua you reign
You are on the
throne

I am
not alone
Your love
is like the warmth
of the sun

i rejoice
in revelation

sometimes
You give a glimpse
of our world
to
come

"Therefore see, the days are coming," declares YHWH, "when it is no longer said, 'YHWH lives who brought up the children of Yisrael from the land of Egypt.'
but YHWH lives who brought up the children of Yisrael from the land of the north and from all the lands where He had driven them.' For I shall bring them back into their land I gave to their fathers." - Jeremiah 16:14-15

Kosher

Many people refer to vision of Peter to say that God declared all foods clean. But let's take a closer look at what the scripture is saying.

At Caesarea there was a man named Cornelius, a centurion in what was known as the Italian Regiment. He and all his family were devout and God-fearing; he gave generously to those in need and prayed to God regularly. One day at about three in the afternoon he had a vision. He distinctly saw an angel of God, who came to him and, "Cornelius!"

Cornelius stared at him in fear. "What is it, Lord?" he asked.

The angel, "Your prayers and gifts to the poor have come up as a memorial offering before God. Now send men to Joppa to bring back a man named Simon who is called Peter. He is staying with Simon the tanner, whose house is by the sea."

When the angel who spoke to him has gone, Cornelius called two of his servants and devout soldier who

was one of his attendants. He told
them everything that had happened
and sent them to Joppa.
- *Acts 10:1-8*

We start here, because Cornelius
is the reason for Peter's vision.

About noon the following day as
they were on their journey and
approaching the city, Peter went up
on the roof to pray. He became
hungry and wanted something to
eat, and while the meal was being
prepared, he fell into a trance.
He saw heaven opened and
something like a large sheet being let
down to earth by its four corners.
- *Acts 10:9-11*

A closer look at this passage of
Scripture reveals that the "vessel" or
"object" being lowered by four
corners was a tallit (or prayer
shawl).

The Tanak frequently uses the
phrase 'four corners' to symbolize

the world. The Hebrew word KANFOT which means CORNERS is also used to describe the wings of angels which resemble human beings (in Ezekiel 1:28a). the tallit or prayer shawl also has four corners to which the tzit tzit fringes are attached.

Wearing a tzit tzit is commanded for ALL GOD'S PEOPLE in both Deuteronomy 22:12 and Numbers 15:37-41. Once again, the Torah (or wedding contract) is the Constitution of the Kingdom. No one is exempt from this.

He saw heaven opened and something like a large sheet being let down to earth by it's four corners. It contained all kinds of four-footed animals, as well as reptiles and birds. Then a voice told him, "Get up, Peter. Kill and eat."
*   - Acts 10:11-13*

What we have here is an instance of Divine Sarcasm. God has a sense of humor. Let's rewind to a similar instance with Ezekiel (Ezekiel 4:12-15).

Eat the food as you would a loaf of barley bread; bake it in the sight of the people, using human excrement for fuel. "The Lord said," in this way the people of Israel will eat defiled food among the nations where I will drive them."

Then I said, "Not so, Sovereign Lord! I have never defiled myself. From my youth until now I have never eaten anything found dead or torn by wild animals. No impure meat has ever entered my mouth."

"Very well," he said, "I will let you bake your bread over a cow dung instead of human excrement."

-Ezekiel 4:12-15

It is not clear that this is sarcasm? Let us continue...

"Surely not, Lord!" Peter replied, I have never eaten anything impure or unclean."

The voice spoke to him a second time, "Do not call anything impure that God has made clean."

- Acts 10:14-15

YHWH was evoking Peter's knowledge of the Torah to make a point: YHWH has not created the Gentile "unclean." That was a rabbinic fabrication. When it came to the Gentiles, Peter was to follow the written Torah, not the rabbis.

YHWH was sending Cornelius (a Gentile) to Peter but needed to diffuse Peter's belief that Gentile's were unfit for fellowship because there was something Peter had to do.

This happened three times, and immediately the sheet was taken back to heaven.

While Peter was wondering about the meaning of the vision, the men sent by Cornelius found out where Simon's house was an stopped at the gate. They called out, asking if Simon who was known as Peter was staying there.

While Peter was still thinking about the vision, the Spirit said to him, "Simon, three men are looking for you. So get up and go downstairs. Do not hesitate to go with them for I have sent them."

Peter went down and said to the men, "I'm the one you're looking for. Why have you come?"

The men replied, "We have come from Cornelius the centurion. He is a righteous and God-fearing man, who is respected by all the Jewish people. A holy angel told him to ask you to come to his house so that he could hear what you have to say." Then Peter invited the men into the house to be his guests.

    -   *Acts 10:16-23*

Peter then goes on to confess the following to them:

You are well aware that it is against our law for a Jew to associate with or visit a Gentile. But God has shown me that I should not call anyone impure or unclean."
- *Acts 10:28*

Peter understood the purpose of the vision had nothing to do with food.

"I now realize how true it is that God does not show favoritism but accepts from every nation the one who fears Him and does what is right.
- *Acts 10:34-35*

The Tzitzit (four corners of the world) represents all those who have been GRAFTED-INTO the kingdom (Romans 11:13-25). It's all about us being the bride and Yeshua/Jesus being the groom. He is not only the commandments-int the flesh-He is the reason to obey the commandments; nor can we obey them without Him.

This means: EVERYBODY (not just the Jewish people-who by the way are only those from the region of Judah).

This righteousness is given through faith in Jesus Christ to all who believe. There is no difference between Jew and Gentile, for all have sinned and fall short of the glory of God.
> - *Romans 3:22-23*

So do we, or do we not believe the Scriptures?

Or is God the God of the Jews only? Is He not the God of the Gentiles too, since there is only one God, who will justify the circumcised by faith and the uncircumcised through that same faith. Do we, then, nullify the law by this faith? Not at all! Rather, we uphold the law.
> - *Romans 3:29-31*

You cannot separate the Torah (wedding contract) from the Groom-

Living Torah; they are one and the same.

If you were Abraham's children, "said Jesus, "*then you would do what Abraham did. As it is, you are looking for a way to kill me, a man who has told you the truth that I heard from God. Abraham did not do such things.*
  -   John 8:39-40

God told Abraham to take his son, his only son...

It is not as though God's word had failed. For not all who are descended from Israel are Israel. Nor because they are his descendants are they all Abraham's children. On the contrary, "It is through Isaac that your offspring will be reckoned." In other words, it is not the children by physical descent who are God's children, but it is the children of promise who are regarded as Abraham's offspring.
  -   Romans 9:6-8

The children of Abraham (the children of the promise) are those saved by the blood of Jesus.

Then they went home and prepared spices and perfumes. But they rested on the Sabbath in obedience to the Commandment.

- Luke 23:56

What is Kosher?

Kosher means fit or proper; appropriate, genuine, legitimate.

Remember, that the very first sin involved Adam and Eve eating something they were not supposed to eat. And we were cursed as a result.

As we have shown in the previous chapter, God has not declared all foods clean.

It is customary to say a blessing before eating, but the fact is…if we are following the commandments (eating kosher) there is already a blessing attached to that food.

If you are not eating kosher, well then you best say a blessing for sure. But understand, it's not a matter of saying magical words. Many diseases and health problems arise from our digesting food which was not meant for our bodies to digest.

So, let's looks at what the Scriptures say as to what is kosher, and what is not. Also, let's look at how Messianics (Messiah-believing) kosher eaters interpret these, Scriptures.

For you are a people holy [set apart] to YHWH your Elohim. Out of all the peoples on the face of the earth, YHWH has chosen you to be His treasured possession. Do not eat any of detestable thing. These are the animals you may eat: the ox, the sheep, the goat, the deer, the gazelle, the roe deer, the wild goat, the ibex, the antelope and the mountain sheep. You may eat animal that has a split hoof divided in two and that chews the cud. However, of those that chew the cud or that have a split hoof completely divided you may not eat the camel, the rabbit or the coney. Although they chew the cud, they do not have a split hoof. The pig is unclean: although it has a split hoof, it does not chew the cud. You are not to eat their meat or touch their carcasses. Of all the creatures living in the water, you may eat any that has fins and scales. But anything that does not have fins and scales you may not eat: for it is unclean. You may eat any clean bird. But these you may not eat: the eagle, the vulture, the black vulture, the red kite, the black kite,

any kind of falcon, any kind of raven, the horned owl, the screech owl, the gull, the white owl, the desert owl, the osprey, the cormorant, the stork, any kind of heron, the hoopoe and the bat. All flying insects that swarm are unclean to you; do not eat them. But any winged creature that is clean you may eat. Do not eat anything you find already dead. You may give it to an alien living in any of your towns, and he may eat it, or you may sell it to a foreigner. But you are a people holy to YHWH Elohim. Do not cook a young goat in its mother's milk.

- *Deuteronomy 14:2-21*

More of the Scriptural Dietary
Instructions.

*Among the animals, whatever
divides the hoof, having cloven
hooves and chewing the cud—that
you may eat. Nevertheless these you
shall not eat among those that chew
the cud or those that have cloven
hooves: the camel, because it chews
the cud but does not have cloven
hooves, is [a]unclean to
you; the [b]rock hyrax, because it
chews the cud but does not have
cloven hooves, is [c]unclean to
you; the hare, because it chews the
cud but does not have cloven
hooves, is unclean to you; and the
swine, though it divides the hoof,
having cloven hooves, yet does not
chew the cud, is unclean to
you. Their flesh you shall not eat,
and their carcasses you shall not
touch. They are unclean to
you. 'These you may eat of all
that are in the water: whatever in the
water has fins and scales, whether*

in the seas or in the rivers—that you may eat. But all in the seas or in the rivers that do not have fins and scales, all that move in the water or any living thing which is in the water, they are [d]an abomination to you. They shall be an abomination to you; you shall not eat their flesh, but you shall regard their carcasses as an abomination. Whatever in the water does not have fins or scales—that shall be an abomination to you. 'And these you shall regard as an abomination among the birds; they shall not be eaten, they are an abomination: the eagle, the vulture, the buzzard, the kite, and the falcon after its kind; every raven after its kind, the ostrich, the short-eared owl, the sea gull, and the hawk after its kind; the little owl, the fisher owl, and the screech owl; the white owl, the jackdaw, and the carrion vulture; the stork, the heron after its kind, the hoopoe, and the bat. 'All flying insects that creep on all fours shall be an abomination to you. Yet these you may eat of

*every flying insect that creeps
on all fours: those which have jointed
legs above their feet with which to
leap on the earth. These you may
eat: the locust after its kind, the
destroying locust after its kind, the
cricket after its kind, and the
grasshopper after its kind. But
all other flying insects which have
four feet shall be an abomination to
you. 'By these you shall
become [e]unclean; whoever touches
the carcass of any of them shall be
unclean until evening; whoever
carries part of the carcass of any of
them shall wash his clothes and be
unclean until evening: The carcass of
any animal which divides the foot,
but is not cloven-hoofed or does not
chew the cud, is unclean to you.
Everyone who touches it shall be
unclean. And whatever goes on its
paws, among all kinds of animals
that go on all fours,
those are unclean to you. Whoever
touches any such carcass shall be
unclean until evening. Whoever
carries any such carcass shall wash*

his clothes and be unclean until evening. It is unclean to you. 'These also shall be unclean to you among the creeping things that creep on the earth: the mole, the mouse, and the large lizard after its kind; the gecko, the monitor lizard, the sand reptile, the sand lizard, and the chameleon. These are unclean to you among all that creep.

Whoever touches them when they are dead shall be unclean until evening…

'And every creeping thing that creeps on the earth shall be [h]an abomination. It shall not be eaten. Whatever crawls on its belly, whatever goes on all fours, or whatever has many feet among all creeping things that creep on the earth—these you shall not eat, for they are an abomination. You shall not make [i]yourselves [i]abominable with any creeping thing that creeps; nor shall you make yourselves unclean with them, lest you be defiled by them. For I am the Lord your God. You shall

*therefore consecrate yourselves,
and you shall be holy; for I am holy.
Neither shall you defile yourselves
with any creeping thing that creeps
on the earth. For I am the Lord who
brings you up out of the land of
Egypt, to be your God. You shall
therefore be holy, for I am holy.
'This is the law [k]of the animals and
the birds and every living creature
that moves in the waters, and of
every creature that creeps on the
earth, to distinguish between the
unclean and the clean, and between
the animal that may be eaten and
the animal that may not be eaten.' "*

- *Leviticus 11:1-32, 41-47*

YHWH also forbids the consumption of blood.

*And wherever you live, you must
not eat the blood of any bird or
animal. Anyone who eats blood must
be cut off from their people.'"*
- *Leviticus 7:26-27*

This is because life is in blood. It is the blood that makes atonement for the soul. Hence, the reason why the shedding of Yeshua's blood saves us.

'And whatever man of the house of Yisrael, or of the strangers who dwell among you, who eats any blood, I will set My face against that person who eats blood, and will cut him off from among his people. For the life of the flesh is in the blood, and I have given it to you upon the altar to make atonement for your souls; for it is the blood that makes atonement for the soul.' Therefore I said to the children of Yisrael, 'No one among you shall eat blood, nor shall any stranger who dwells among you eat blood.'
- *Leviticus 17:10-12*

Let's consider the discovery of microscopic sub-cellular, seemingly indestructible particles, called "somatids." It means: Tiny particle. Somatids are much smaller than cells, and can remain alive for centuries. Blood may dry up at times it may appear to be dead but there is still life within it. Since blood always contains somatids – you are in fact- eating the life of another being. It is easy to see how this can be the cause of many health problems.

Traditional "Jewish" weddings take place under a "chupah," which is a tallit (prayer shawl) held above the Groom and Bride on the four corners. With this covering of the tallit, they are symbolizing that their marriage will be under the protection and authority of YHWH.

"...your time was the time of love, and I spread my mantle over you and covered your nakedness. And I swore an oath to you and entered into a covenant with you, and you became Mine..."
- *Ezekiel 16:8*

In Peter's vision, the Gentiles are healed or lowered into the fold by the Great Shepard from above by His tzitzit which brings healing to all the nations and we can see the grafting in, or joining between Gentile converts and native Yisraelites.

children of the promise

i am on my way back
to the land of the living
Yeshua is
the forgiving
where the end
meets the beginning

i am stuck
like glue
to those afternoons
and days that
end too soon
moments in tune
with songs of deliverance

i know that YHWH
has a plan
too obvious to understand
when He calls for me
here i am

i believe
half of what i see
only if it is spiritually
discerned
am i able to learn

His blood
He has given
people of the way
He is risen
His life in exchange for

eden restored

baptized with fire

only YHWH can make a man
He doesn't make suggestions
He commands
like a father
who understands
that iron sharpens iron

love is not a feeling
love is spiritual
water into wine
is a miracle
refined
in the fire
i take in
breath
from the four winds

YHWH is in the pain
the sweet thoughts
of the rain
these times
they test my faith
weakness
doesn't like to wait

spiritual warfare
love versus hate

it is written
that the Word
of the Elohim
comes not
to bring peace

but a sword

dominion

you can keep running
like Jonah
a belly of the fish
type persona
cause when you don't
forgive
you will live with
the tormentors

beauty is on
the inside
when you abide
in Him
not when you
encourage sin

he shall have
dominion
YHWH is not a man
that He should lie
those are bad soul ties

the Kingdom of Elohim
is now
the truth will find a way
somehow
you'll see

you suffer with Him
you reign with Him

doing what is right
is
worth the cost

that's the jumpoff

so tighten up
in His word
we trust
faith is a must

forgiveness is a decision

back when
your heart
was open
when your smile
told a story
i made a promise
to the wind

gave YHWH the glory
on a whim

i sought
safe haven
in
the color
of your eyes

now
to her surprise
receding sunrise
i hold a
vanished
shadow

may her coming days
outshine
the haze
Elohim of
New Jerusalem
i pray

because
i am so very
sorry

one day
of His light
lasts
a thousand years

i hope that
we
can dry
the tears

For I will take you out of the nations, I will gather you from all the countries and bring you back into your land. I will throw clean water on you, and you will be clean. I will cleanse you from all your impurities and from all your idols. I will give you a new heart and put a new spirit in you. I will remove from you your heart of stone and give you a heart of flesh. And I will put my Spirit in you and move you to follow my decrees and be careful to keep my Torah."

- Ezekiel 36:24-27

The origin of Halloween

From The Book of Holidays, 1958, by J. Walker McSpadden, pages 149-153:

Halloween – in spite of the fact that it takes its name from a Christian festival (All Hallows or All Saint's Day), comes from pagan times and has never taken on a Christian significance.

On that night between October and November, the Druids kindled great fires on the hills as a barrier against the evil to come. (These Halloween fires still burn every year in many places, but especially in Scotland and Wales). By waving burning wisps of plaited straw aloft on pitchforks, people tried to frighten off demons and witches, but just in case this didn't work, they also put on grotesque and terrifying costumes. For if you dressed in a horrible enough fashion and went trooping around with the spirits all night, they would think you were one of them, and do you no harm. This is where the persistent

Halloween custom of "dressing up" and wearing masks originated.

In The Book of Festival Holidays, 1964, by Marguerite Ickis, Pages 123-125

The last day of the year on the old pagan calendar, October 31, served the triple purpose of bidding goodbye to summer, welcoming winter, and remembering the dead.

Folks began hollowing out turnips and pumpkins and placing lighted candles inside to scare evil spirits from the house.

Why was the result called a "jack-o'-lantern"? Tradition says that an Irish Jack, too wicked for heaven and expelled from hell for playing tricks on the devil, was condemned to walk the earth with a lantern forever.

It was the Irish, who initiated the "trick or treat" system hundreds of years ago.

Halloween scarcely observed in the United States until the last half of the nineteenth century. It is thought the large-scale Irish immigration had much to do with the popularizing of the holiday.

A prophecy in the Tanak speaks of the Messiah: The Sun of Righteousness shall arise with healing in His wings. Malachi 4:2 NKJV

These "wings" are "kanaph" in Hebrew, and refer to the edge of a garment, which is the tzitzit. We read in the Gospel according to Luke: *"Now a woman, having a flow of blood for twelve years, who had spent all her livelihood on physicians and could not be healed by any, came from behind and touched the border of His garment. And immediately her flow of blood stopped."* – Luke 8:43-44 NKJV

The Greek word used to describe a border is "kraspedon" which means a fringe or tassel. In other words, she grabbed His tzitzit that He was wearing in obedience to the Torah. Therefore, He came with healing in His tzitzit just as was foretold by the prophet Malachi.

Also, in Matthew 14:35-36 we read: *And when the men of that place (Gennesar) recognized Him, they sent out into all that surrounding country, and brought to Him all who were sick, and begged Him to let them only touch the tzitzit of His garment. And as many as touched it were completely healed."*

December 25th

From the Pagan-Christian Connection exposed by Michael Rood, page 79.

At the time of Winter Solstice, December 25th on the ancient calendar, they had a public child mass [mass meaning "sacrifice"]. The priests stoked the iron image of the enthroned chemosh with wood and burning pitch. Turning their pot-bellied god into a cherry red furnace. The people made long lists of their desires, and recited them to the god of prosperity just before they put their infant children into the red-hot lap of their god with his phrygian cap. As the babies were incinerated in the December 25th child mass, the people were assured that their sacrifices would be rewarded in the coming year.

On the same day, south of Israel, the Egyptians worshipped their sun god, Ra. An Egyptian hieroglyph depicts Ra castrating himself-the same act that Greek mythology attributes to Attis. Worshippers of Ra would hang gold and silver balls on an upright palm tree, as the prophet Jeremiah reports, and place their decorated gifts to the sun god under the tree adorned with gold and silver testicles of Ra (Jeremiah 10:1-5). This vain custom was performed on Ra's birthday – December 25th. When Israel adopted this custom, they used the evergreen tree, which they cut out of the forest with an axe and erected in their homes with the help of a hammer and nails so that it would not topple over. Finally, they decked it with gold and silver balls. The Almighty calls this festival "an abomination." In the 1600s it was illegal to have a christmas tree or even a christmas service, in America. The pilgrims knew that is was pure pagan sun god worship.

We read in the scroll of Ruth that Elimelech and his family left Bethlehem during a drought and sojourned east of Israel in the land of Moab. The Moabites were worshippers of Chemosh, the pagan god of prosperity. It was the same cast-iron, pot-bellied god that their kindred, the Ammonites, worshipped by the name of Molech. Both gods wore the phrygian cap the official headwear of both Tammuz in Babylon, and later Mithra in Rome.

At the time of the Winter Solstice, December 25th on the ancient calendar, they had a public mass [mass meaning "sacrifice."] As the babies were incinerated, the people were assured their long lists of desires would be rewarded in the coming year.

Was Jesus only a Prophet?

Now this was John's testimony when the Jewish leaders in Jerusalem sent priests and Levites to ask him who he was. He did not fail to confess, but confessed freely, "I am not the Messiah."

They asked him, "Then who are you? Are you Elijah?" He said "I am not."
"Are you the Prophet?"
He answered, "No."
Finally they said, "Who are you? Give us an answer to take back to those who sent us. What do you say about yourself?"
John replied in the words of Isaiah the prophet, "I am the voice of one calling in the wilderness, make straight the way of the Lord." – John 1:19-23

Now many look to John the Baptist's words in this passage to place the name of whatever - prophet- they see fit in his explanation of who he's not.

But if we are going to look at John's words let's be consistent. John never -at any time- referred to Jesus as only a prophet. If indeed, Jesus -or anyone else- was the "prophet," John would surely have confessed this. John only said that he was the voice crying in the wilderness to prepare people for the coming of the Messiah. But he did know -from birth- that he would go in the spirit and power of Elijah (Luke1:17). Remember, John was the only one qualified to pronounce that Jesus was the Lamb of God being that he was from the same line as Aaron (as son of Zechariah).

The disciples asked him, "why then do the teachers of the law say that Elijah must come first?"
Jesus replied, "To be sure, Elijah comes and will restore all things. But I tell you Elijah has already come, and they did not recognize him, but have done to him everything they wished. In the same way the Son of Man is going to suffer at their

hands." Then the disciples
understood that He was talking
about John the Baptist.
        - Matthew 17:10-13

    John the Baptist was "the spirit
of Elijah" or "that prophet" (Elijah
was a prophet). The Hebrew word for
prophet is NABI.
    The spirit of Elijah is spoken of
again in Malachi:

See, I am sending you Elijah "the
prophet" before the coming of the
great and awesome day of YHWH.
    -   Malachi 4:5

    This is the spirit which is active
in the world right now. It is restoring
the worship of the Messiah back to
its original state before it was
corrupted by the Roman Empire.
This is because He is returning soon
    There are some who delight in
bashing Christians for their pagan
practices. I, however, am not one of
these people. I attend Christian
services (as well as Messianic). What

I do, I do in love as there does need to be an awakening in Christianity.

It's like I always say: sometimes Christians need more Yeshua, and Messianics need more Jesus. Both are a people committed to their Savior.

Christians have a deep passion for the Messiah; it is infectious. What we do, we must do in love.

book of the living

i come from the pits
of deep darkness to tell you
sons of destruction
who become
warriors of light
have defeated the night

Elohim sent lightning
from His right hand
He struck
the shadow of death
kept the fire brands
left

tears wept into steel
bruises were all
i could feel
on the day
we were sealed

a door in heaven
revealed
a sea of glass
the day of the YHWH
came fast

the first generation
must die
don't let the blue sky
fool you

the end is coming

blessed be the merciful

so now
you need mercy
it's time to kneel
you like the way
it feels
when your feet
rush into evil

when YHWH asked you
to forgive
you weren't
interested

but will you
be able
to take the heat
when the devil
sifts you like wheat

have a seat
your maker
will see you
at His earliest
convenience

blood covenant

Yeshua
You are the
incorruptible seed
the eternal vine
in me

keeper of eternity
voice of the light
within
You spin the world
i hold on

designer of the dawn
O Elohim of Israel
Heavenly Father of forever
the harvest of man
is almost complete
You are ready to reap
darkness cannot
see defeat

Holy Spirit
You are
the living truth
the words of Yeshua
in red
the first born from the dead

miami rain

He it is
who makes the clouds rise
where the
guardian
of my
soul abides
in every moment
to come

the mighty One
of Jacob
is already there
He knew
what I would ask
and more
before He set the world
on its foundation
He saved me
from myself

the riches of His grace
shine brighter
than the miami sun
His mercy comes
like the seabreeze
He will send it
where ever He pleases

O YHWH my Elohim
i will praise You
for every ray of sunshine
i will praise You
for every drop of rain

for You cool
the relentless heat
You hold back the
winds from the south
and you
prepare the way

You know the last prayer
i will pray
You knew each day
before the world began
so my feet
know where to land

You O YHWH
were already here
dear to me
even in the storm
i can see You
commanding
the rain drops

pains of childbirth

that's right
i remember now
how i
played a part
in this disaster

not sure how
i got here
only that it was
meant to be
and only YHWH
can set me free

there is this me
and the me in
eternity

for what is
was
and has been
YHWH is not
trapped in
time
He never was

we hope
for what we do not see
the whole creation
the first generation

death means
re-birth
after the first fruits
of the spirit
YHWH will reveal
eternity future

Yeshua sent these twelve out, having
commanded them, saying, "Do not go into the
way of the gentiles, and do not enter a city of the
Shomeronites.
but rather go to the lost sheep of Yisrael.
And as you go, proclaim, saying, 'The reign of
the heavens has drawn near.'
                    -Matthew 10:6

robe of light

there i was
on the edge of hope
about to fall
graffiti on the wall
broken pieces
of yesterday

in His loving way
He beat me down
it is there
He can be found
He descended
down
where
nothing is left
but
destruction and death
shortness of breath
and He finds a
shining star
we are the
depths
of His mercy

those who are forgiven
the most
love the most
said the host of heaven

and He
opened a door
no more
was i
the object of wrath
He paved the
path
to the Holy place

He will
fill
the moon with blood
the sun
He will unplug

there will
be no where to run
wisdom
is justified
of all her children

bricks of the fallen

the bricks have fallen
but
what will you rebuild?
it is the YHWH
you better fear

the last hour
is here
and were you warned?
with great heat
you were scorned

the fowls
will be filled
with their flesh
their destiny
is destruction

when you
took prayer
out of schools
they became
a sesspool

the blind guides
who hide
from the light
your enemy
will smite you

you will flee
to the children
of the free
woman
the city
of the great whore
will burn
forevermore
and the
prayers of the saints
will rain
like seeds

faith
with good deeds
alone
will please
Him
on the throne

corridor

the key of David
will cease
as far as the vine
can reach
parameters teach my
feet where to go

only the
fear of the YHWH
can enter
the corridor
the thoughts of
the flesh are clear
when suffering
is near
they retreat
until dread is complete

follow your feet
of discernment
to find a door
there is more
you must overcome
it is done
if you find a way
in YHWH's will

in the regions dark

the green of the trees
have a dark shade
these are
the days
that the rain has made
vision is blurred
clouds like a skull
the
falling
drops
feel like bleeding
and the cool breeze
is deceiving

i do
what i can
what a wretched man
i am
undercover for YHWH
no changing
the plan now
that i can
hear the wind
howl

when He draws near
darkness disappears
the evil will choke
they will vanish
like smoke

i can hear
the mouths
of the grave
calling
my
name

temblar de miedo

if YHWH
can't control me
no one can

prison
can only hold the body
the spirit still has power

when you fear YHWH
something changes
wisdom is born
the spiritual realm
begins to form
like the wind
you don't know
where you're goin

watch the horizon fall
when YHWH turns
it all upside down
it's time to hit
the ground
running

entrance to the Kingdom

fishers of men
feed my sheep
enter by the door
keep the entrance
forming
according
to your call

words should
have all meaning
acts will
be redeeming
faith with a leap
most of all
feed my sheep

confirm your call
do not fall asleep
pray you feed
my sheep
most assuredly

do you love me?

**And He answering, said, "I was not sent except
to the lost sheep of the house of Yisrael."
- Matthew 15:24**

repent

knocked down
but turned
back around
pressing
forward
rising
to the occasion
finding the equation

stronger than before
one more answer
to give
helping the dead
to live
a multitude of sins
gone with the wind

fruit
worthy of repentence
reversal
of a sentence
to turn away
to see another day

faith is no more

than what you say
godly sorrow
changes the way
of your mind

for though
a righteous man
falls
seven times

he rises again

transmitted power

underneath
huge rear wings
sport-racing
coil springs
keep my
wheels spinning

He put
my dog clutch
to the test
constant-mesh
straight-cut
spur gears
i left
behind the years

for we are
His workmanship
created in
Yeshua
for good works

just like the sun
brings the bling
i'm engaging the asphalt
ripping
off the rubber
my thundercloud
is heaven sent
power is in the present

introjection

information
repeated
over time
will
penetrate the mind

manifest reactions
once emergent
destructive acts
insurgence

when the wheels
in your head
turn deadly
consider a
carefully
planned
ego deviation
an infusive invasion
the pulling down
of strongholds
salvation

the opposite
of the flesh
a spiritual
perspective
edification
a greater degree
of observation

torpedo junction

ohh USA
let YHWH
do it His way
you are too young
to know
He runs the show
YHWH of Hosts

it's a done deal
your faith is a shield
bullets
flying in all directions
like Rangers in Vietnam
YHWH takes out
who He wants
at will
some
to fill the pit
some make it

but terrorism
i don't understand
come out
and fight like a man

fighting an enemy
we can't see
sounds like
a spiritual war

if four
unarmed chaplains
at the junction can speak
for the YHWH

what do they
need to hide for?

"I am the good shepherd. And I know Mine, and Mine know Me, even as the Father knows Me, and I know the Father. And I lay down My life for the sheep.
"And the other sheep I have which are not of this fold - I have to bring them as well, and they shall hear My voice, and there shall be one flock, one Shepherd."
- John 10:14-16

lukewarm

YHWH is gonna
use you
so are you hot
or cold?

how is your story told?
to which path
have you sold out?
whether you oppress
to impress
or you ride
with the blessed
do it
with all your might

because you can't
do both and do right
either burn with Nero
or play the hero

but stay out
the middle of the road

sense of mission

a cool feather
hair flip
is not gonna
do it
stressed
to the extreme
the command
climate mean

freedom fighting
not faith-based
stay out of the way
you cannot say
fight wrong
with more wrong
those days are gone
only YHWH
can fight evil

landfall

80 degrees at 6 a.m.
tropical depression
number eleven
my clinical
observation
is that it's
an isolated shower
flash flooding
storm surge
a little tense
like
cognitive dissonance
coming
your way
red-flag delays
anti-lock brakes
save the day

the USA
has forgotten
YHWH's warning
it's not global
warming
He has turned
up the heat
we are in
the hot seat

the cup of salvation

i drank away the black
YHWH
is not slack concerning
His promise
He bruises
But He binds up

the accuser
of the brethren
swallowed up
by the cup of salvation
the devil
of the flood
who tried
to prevent the birth
will be
digested
by the earth

the eternal king
our advocate
for
everything
from which
the eight souls
were saved
He forgave

sons of the living El

we are
the one
clothed with the sun
one spirit
one body in Yeshua
all in one accord
temple
of the sword

one caused the fall
so one died for all
the bridegroom awaits
for who
YHWH has called
He will join together

do you know
yet
who you have decided?
for we were
bought with a price
blood
the atoning sacrifice

He foreknew
what we would choose
it all
had to happen once
He's already
known us
children
of the promise

Then He went down to Capernaum, a town in Galilee, and on the Sabbath He taught the people.

- **Luke 4:31**

One thing that is important to realize: You do
not translate a name - you transliterate names,
which means that you pronounce them the same
in different languages.
There is no "J" sound in Hebrew.

unity of the Spirit

i am a Father
a brother
and a son
all
at the same time
together
unity of mind
as for example
mankind

as a result
of Yeshua
we have one hope
one Elohim
of all
just as we were
called
one spirit
one body

just as one
brought us
into sin
one
brought us out

climate change summit

the devil
wants you
to believe
it's global warming

the deception is forming

greenhouse gases
carbon emissions
desperate decisions

the energy
the enemy
has spent
he doesn't want you
to repent

YHWH's Judgments
have not went
well
discernment
is a hard sell

easier for the
nations to tell
you
a lie

than to admit
the
end is nigh

hija mia

querria que no
hubiera pasado
nunca

si vieras como
ha cambiado
todo aquello

me duele

se vertiran muchas
lagrimas
por esto

yo te leia cuentos

nos reiamos mucho

te quiero

i love the way you prove your love

i love the way
you prove your love
it's your heart
the way you lean
on YHWH
for strength

you take your stand
when most
don't understand
that life
demands
a level
of moral reason

some things
may be legal
but they are immoral
there is a way
that seems
right
but leads to death

you leave me
breathless

my mother's love

mothers are
what it means to
be committed

they are
compassionately
connected
unconditional
receptive

a love
chosen
to last

purple

she did
not let go
so easy
in the end
the one
to please me
was my
friend

nor do i
send
regrets
but acceptance
for the
chance
to love
forever

hearts of gold
can never
sever
what
it meant
nor could i
mend it
so i must amend it
then i
let it go

did you think
i would
not
sew
these threads
when cooler heads
prevail
forgiveness tells
the tale

purple
is the trail
and YHWH will never fail

to bless the broken road

He went to Nazareth, where He had been brought up, and on the Sabbath day he went into the synagogue, as was his custom. He stood up to read…

- Luke 4:16

Lost Sheep

Ekklesia means set apart assembly, congregation. Ekklesia in the Renewed Testament never meant a building or house called a Church. The true assembly consists of the Body of Yeshua.

And He said, "Because of this I have said to you that no one is able to come to Me unless it has been given to him by My Father."
- John 6:65

YHWH has to open the person's eyes; there is no other way. People have put up walls, due to false doctrine. Sometimes it is as simple as Truth vs. Tradition. Embracing the Torah for some, could mean giving up Christmas and Easter. How would the person explain this to his/her family? Or several generations of his/her family have been preachers (all of one denomination) and they feel pressured to continue in these teachings. The traditions of these teachings override their ability to receive the truth.

Sometimes an Anti-Semitic spirit is at work; telling the person it's a Jewish thing. You are only Jewish if you are from Judah. And ethnicity won't save you. Anyone can be grafted into the Kingdom (Romans 11:17-22).

In ancient Egypt, many were saved by the Blood of the Lamb (Yeshua's Blood). YHWH proceeded to part the Red Sea for them. But most of these people still died in the wilderness; because they did not follow the wedding contract (The Torah).

And all the people gathered together and said, "All that YHWH has spoken we shall do." So Moses brought back the words of the people to YHWH.
-Exodus 19:8

This was the day we said "I do"

to the wedding proposal. If Yeshua was going to abandon the wedding contract, He might as well abandon the wedding. Think of the Torah as the Constitution of the Kingdom. Anyone who lives by it IS THE SET APART ASSEMBLY. It has nothing to do with a brick or mortar building.

Still there are some that insist that Yeshua did away with the Torah by fulfilling it. He also fulfilled baptism, but we still get baptised.

Then Yeshua came from Galil to John at the Garden to be baptised by him.
But John was hindering Him, saying "I need to be baptised by You, and You come to me?"
But Yeshua answering, said to him, "Permit it now, for thus it is fitting for us to fulfill all righteousness." Then he permitted him.
- Matthew 3:13-15

There it is, right there: by getting baptised, Yeshua fulfilled all righteousness. It surely sounds to me like He fulfilled baptism. So then, we don't need to get baptised then; because he fulfilled it? right? The answer is: No. That is ridiculous, right? The problem is people believe we can pick and choose what we still have to do and what we don't have to do.

One of the reasons we call it - The Messianic Movement - is because if everyone is doing as He did; it should be ONE MOVEMENT. It eliminates the need for many denominations (and their bitter rivalries). It's not just the Words in red (what he said), it's the Words in black (what He did). If He did it, we ought to do it. It's just that simple. And anyone who tells you different is a liar.

He lived the Torah, I live the Torah. He got baptised, I get baptised. He observed Sabbath, I observe Sabbath. He went by the Lunar Calendar and observed the Appointed Times. Therefore, I will. It should be ONE MOVEMENT. Otherwise, there is a disconnect. And I know it hurts to know we've been lied to. But the devil deceived the whole world; not just us. And it's time we get over it.

We are told in the Scriptures that the reason The Houses of Israel and Judah were exiled was because of their failure to obey the Torah. Furthermore, the prophecies tell us that the Covenant involves the Torah being written on our hearts and in our minds and that the Messiah will rule according to the Torah and teach us the Torah from Zion (Isaiah 2:1-4 Micah 4:1-5).

"Do not think that I came to destroy the Torah or the Prophets. I did not come to destroy but to fulfill. For assuredly, I say to you, till heaven and earth pass away, one jot or one tittle will by no means pass

from the Torah till all is fulfilled. Whoever therefore breaks one of the least of these commandments, and teaches men so, shall be called least in the kingdom of heaven but whoever does and teaches them, he shall be called great in the kingdom of heaven."
- Matthew 5:17-19

The mere fact that the Holy Spirit wrote this Scripture, is evidence that there is a disconnect (that Scriptures which appear to contradict this are either accidental or blatant misinterpretations). And in fact, much is lost in translation once it hits the page in English. To get the pure cut, meaning of the Scriptures you've got to go to the original language in which it was written.

The one who came to kill, steal, and destroy is the devil, not Yeshua. Yeshua wouldn't destroy the Torah.

The Word "fulfill" comes from the Greek word: PLEROSAI. PLEROSAI means to "fill up, to fully preach, to make full, to make complete." The Greek word KATALOOSAI means "destroy, dissolve, or demolish." KATALOOSAI is not the word used. PLEROSAI is the word used. Yeshua said "until heaven and earth pass away" not the smallest portion of the Torah will pass away. This is easily observable. Does anyone believe that heaven and earth has passed away?

From Perga they went on to Pisidian Antioch. On the Sabbath they entered the synagogue and sat down. After the reading from the Law and the Prophets, the leaders of the synagogue sent word to them, saying, "Brothers, if you have a word of exhortation for the people, please speak."

- Acts 13:14-15

Neither Christianity nor Judaism existed
when Yeshua ministered on the Earth.
He and His disciples taught and obeyed
the Torah. Neither did Yeshua or His
disciples create or convert to
Christianity. Christianity was created by
The Roman Empire and became their
state religion.

The Next Exodus

The next Exodus is often called "The Greater Exodus."

"And I shall bring you out from the peoples and gather you out of the lands where you are scattered, with a mighty hand, and with an outstretched arm, and with wrath poured out.
And I shall bring you into the wilderness of the peoples, and shall enter into judgment with you face to face there.
As I entered into judgment with your fathers in the wilderness of the land of Egypt, so I shall enter into judgment with you, declares the Adon YHWH."
- Ezekiel 20:34-36

There will be a face-to-face judgment with YHWH in the wilderness just as there was the first time. History will repeat itself.

"Remember this and show yourselves men turn it back you

transgressors.
Remember the former of long ago,
for I am El, and there is no one else
- Elohim, and there is no one like
Me,
declaring the end from the
beginning, and from of old that
which has not been done, saying,
'My counsel stands, and all My
delight I do.' "
- Isaiah 46:8-10

If you want to know the end, go back to the beginning. It is all going to repeat itself: 1) Two Witnesses (only instead of Moses and Aaron) it will be two other witnesses. 2) Judgments. Only instead of ten judgments on Egypt, there will be 21 judgments (7 seals, 3 judgments each) on the whole world. 3) Exodus. Instead of an Exodus out of Egypt, this time the Exodus will be from all over the world. Just like the first time, YHWH's people will be exempt from the judgments on the world; but will be subject to the face-to-face judgments which result from not obeying the Torah, while in the wilderness.

You'll remember that during the first Exodus, the carcasses fell; of those who disobeyed the Torah. Paul (filled with The Holy Spirit) addresses the last generation. He warns us NOT TO MAKE THE SAME MISTAKES as those who journeyed through the wilderness during the FIRST EXODUS.

For I do not want you to be ignorant, brothers, that all our fathers were under the cloud, and all passed through the sea,
and all were immersed into Moses in the cloud and in the sea,
and all ate the same spiritual food, and all drank the same spiritual drink. For they drank of that spiritual Rock that followed, and the Rock was Mashiach.
However, with most of them Elohim was not well pleased, for they were laid low in the wilderness.

And these became example for us, so that we should not list after evil, as those indeed lusted.

And do not become idolaters as some of them, as it has been written, "The people sat down to eat and to drink, and stood up to play." Neither should we commit whoring, as some of them did, and in one day twenty-three thousand fell, neither let us try Mashiach, as some of them also tried, and were destroyed by serpents, neither grumble, as some of them also grumbled, and were destroyed by the destroyer.

AND ALL THESE CAME UPON THEM AS EXAMPLES, AND THEY WERE WRITTEN AS A WARNING TO US, ON WHOM THE ENDS OF THE AGES HAVE COME, so that he who thinks he stands, let him take heed lest he fall.
- 1 Corinthians 10:1-12

Fairly straightforward. Don't make the same mistakes they did. Isaiah speaks to the last generation

concerning the next Exodus
(Greater Exodus).

*Then YHWH shall create above
every dwelling place of Mount Zion,
and above her assemblies, a cloud
and smoke by day and the shining
of a flaming fire by night, for over all
the esteem shall be a covering,
and a booth for shade in the
daytime from the heat, for a place of
refuge, and for a shelter from storm
and rain.*
- Isaiah 4:5-6

A booth is a tent or tabernacle.
This was written after the first
Exodus and specifically points to
the next Exodus. Isaiah tells us
that we will once again be moving
from camp to camp. When the
cloud by day and fire by night
moves, we move.

Beginning at Sukkot (where the
first Exodus started), there were 41
camps that the Yisraelites stayed
in, before they entered into the

promised land (Numbers 33). Yeshua was resurrected during the Omer count and ascended into the heaven on Day 41 of the Omer count.

Therefore, if those patterns have future meaning, we may see 41 different camps around the earth while the people are being regathered.

The Feast of Tabernacles (also called Sukkot) is when we commemorate how and when we left Egypt. It's a "set apart rehearsal," our escape plan for the end. Those who have been observing this Appointed Time - as the command says (Lev 23) - know this.

"Watch then at all times, and pray that you be counted worthy to escape all this about to take place, and to stand before the Son of Man."
- Luke 21:36

We want to be praying to be part of The Greater Exodus. Especially, those in prison. The Covenant is your ticket out of there. The following would be one of many Scriptures to pray on. This is one of many Greater Exodus Scriptures:

For I know the plans I am planning for you, ' declares YHWH, 'plans of peace and not of evil, to give you an expectancy and a latter end.
'Then you shall call on Me, and shall come and pray to Me, and I shall listen to you.
'And you shall seek, and shall find Me, when you search for Me with all your heart.
'And I shall be found by you,' declares YHWH, and I SHALL TURN BACK YOUR CAPTIVITY, AND SHALL GATHER YOU FROM ALL THE GENTILES AND FROM ALL THE PLACES WHERE I HAVE DRIVEN YOU, DECLARES YHWH. AND I SHALL BRING YOU BACK TO THE PLACE FROM WHICH I HAVE EXILED YOU.' "
- Jeremiah 29:11-14

But wasn't the Exodus in 1948, when they restored the country of Israel? Answer: that was the House of Judah (only two of the twelve tribes). Judah is only one of two sticks. The other ten tribes (the other stick) is known as Ephraim or Israel and consist of those who have been grafted in all over the world. The kingdom was divided into Ephraim and Judah and both of them broke the covenant. However, as the following Scripture indicates; the kingdom is being restored by the joining of the two sticks.

And the word of YHWH came to me, saying,
"And you, son of man, take a stick for yourself and write on it, 'For Yahudah and for the children of Yisrael, his companions.' Then take another stick and write on it, 'For Yoseph, the stick of Ephrayim, and for all the house of Yisrael, his companions.'

"Then bring them together for yourself into one stick, and they shall become one in your hand.

"And when the children of your people speak to you, saying, 'Won't you show us what you mean by these?'
say to them, 'Thus said the Adon YHWH, "See, I am taking the stick of Yoseph, which is in the hand of Ephrayim, and the tribes of Yisrael, his companions. And I shall give them unto him, with the stick of Yahudah, and make them one stick, and they shall be one in my hands." '

"And the sticks on which you write shall be in your hand before their eyes.

"And speak to them, 'Thus said the Adon YHWH, "See, I am taking the children of Yisrael from among the gentiles, wherever they have gone, and shall gather them from all around, and I shall bring them into their own land.

"And I shall make them one nation in the land, on the mountains of Yisrael. And one sovereign shall be

sovereign over them all, and let them no longer be two nations, and let them no longer be divided into two reigns."
- Ezekiel 37:15-22

Paul told people to imitate him as he imitated the Messiah (1 Corinthians 11:1). Paul taught his congregations The Appointed Times (1 Thess 5:1).

Paul told the Corinthians to observe Passover (1 Corinthians 5:6-8).
The fact that Paul had Timothy circumcised shows that Paul had no problem with a Gentile (the nations) receiving circumcision (Acts 16:3).

Paul said under oath that he kept the instructions of The Torah (Acts 24:14-16 - Acts 25:8 - Romans 7:22).
Paul did as the Messiah did. And we ought to do as the Messiah did. In fact, many claim they do as He did but they do not. Yeshua observed the Sabbath. Yeshua observed the Appointed Times. Yeshua taught the Torah and lived by the Torah. Yeshua wore a Tzitzit. Anyone who claims to do as He did, but does not do these things needs to ask themselves: why? Because somewhere there is a disconnect, or the insertion of a false doctrine.

As Paul and Barnabus were leaving the synagogue, the people invited them to speak further about these things on the next Sabbath.
-    **Acts 13:42**

alter of the heart

earthly spirits
need somewhere to dwell
that's why
hell
is a holding place

the human race
has dominion
in order to gain control
a demon
hijacks a soul

activate the jet fuel
who has bewitched you?
cylinder
may experience
detonation
engine needs more air
you are in the cross-hairs

sin is lawlessness
in three dimensions
your temple an extension
that escapes
conscious
awareness

a skeleton plan
hinging on
manual override
hidden things of darkness
inside

threat warning screen
surging to life
YHWH wills
a thief in the night
into existence

emergency options
the devil
was never your friend
you have reached
the end
of the runway

fly or crash

500 pounds of downforce

i was
filled with pride
fighting
the wrong side
a head-on
collision
incoming
smooth
maneuvering
with
an
extra
shot
of
tequila

peak acceleration
without
a fail-safe
my heart
was in the
wrong place

no one
deserved
the problems i had
my little girl
needs her dad

those black glasses
the tint of doom
a man's house
becomes his tomb

YHWH left room
to forgive
i was sensitive
to His infra-red
the dead sat up
i began to speak
His word
strengthens
the weak

in Him do i trust
He raises the poor
from the dust
the worlds in the words
like spiritual
messengers

one bad day away

police should
face consequences
for their offenses
lawful lies hurt
egos
that cost
more than
they're worth

just ask the culprit
of a hit and run
once
you get caught
you are done
it only took one
bad day
to ruin your life

one day you might
find
that only one
fine line
separates us

in the moshpit for Yeshua

we are the real rebels
the ones
who refuse to die
those on the flip side

light
has been thrown
neural pathways
have grown
solar power
grid-connected
a mind transcended

teeth marks
of time
on our fists
were
comin with the blitz

quiet and peaceful
the combustive mix

the price
has been paid
the ax
is laid
into
the root
of the trees

every knee
shall bow

The Messianic Movement is a return to worship -
the way it was - before The Roman Empire
corrupted it. It involves the spirit of Elijah
restoring all things for the return of the Messiah:
The voice crying the wilderness.

Messianics are believers of Yeshua seeking to
assemble and observe the biblical
commandments.
Messianic Movement is a more appropriate term
than "Messianic Jewish", precisely because you
are only Jewish if you're from Judah. Ethnicity
won't save you. Anyone can be grafted into the
kingdom. Whoever obeys the Torah (the
wedding contract) is part of one body (the bride).

If everyone is doing as He did, there should be
ONE MOVEMENT, without the bitter rivalries
of denominations or religion.

**On the next Sabbath almost the whole city
gathered to hear the word of the Lord.**
- **Acts 13:44**

getting the beat

between self and other
one neuron
talking to another
a genotype discovered

factory-installed
DNA
we are
programmed to pray
a fail safe
for judgment day

not out of
obligation
but transformation
a monoamine
collaboration

the science
in the spiritual
self-transcendence
material

ignition timing measure
peak cylinder pressure
becoming self-aware
launch-control software

spiritual communication

consciousness
is the
vocal platform
of the mind
words of a spiritual kind
communication
that transcends time

accountability
the engine of
the possible
YHWH's will
unstoppable

human existence
before YHWH
as spirit
consciousness
will hear it

exposure to light

Your love is deeper
than the depths of the ocean
You have opened
my soul
with Your key

You O YHWH
take care of me
You think of me
and later
i see it was You

my Eternal Father
has words that move
The Most High
The source
of the intense
my peak experience

presence

how precious it is
to have our Creator
within
the living temple
built for Him
spiritual intimacy
meditation
on His word

to cast our burdens
on YHWH
we read the scripture
more and more
harmony
to the core

it is precisely
this
eternal consciousness

The Greek New Testament replaces the name of Eliyahu (Elijah) with the name of the pagan sun god Helios. Upon inspection of the Greek manuscripts, what you will discover is that the Greek name Helios is put in place of the name Eliyahu.

hija mía

estoy triste porque
no estás
aquí

el cielo está gris

tu sunrisa
me hace
mi mundo más claro

the soul ties of april 7th

indissoluble union
what a soul tie is
wholeness
becomes
two parts of one

the inner lives
that survive
separation
fornication
multiplied
tied
to the motions
of sins

whatever happens
below
the threshold
of awareness

i was a slave
to the flesh
broken by death
one step
away
Yeshua had
the last say

the comforter
who freed me from
my chains
He changed the night
into the light

the carnal man
cannot understand
what is spiritual
demands
that you abandon
the intellect
but not the factual

He put
the
super
on the natural

further down the corridor

it's just not in
the parameters
of YHWH's Will
but there are
still open
doors

there is more
to the
spiritual realm
than i know
though
i cannot see it
i believe this
is a wall
here

but i'm free
to keep
moving
in this direction
pending
further
correction

The pagans called every one of their deities a "christ" which is commonly translated as "anointed." While Yeshua was indeed "anointed" He was not a christ in the pagan sense - He was the Messiah.

Emperor Constantine did worship a christ, although it was not the Hebrew Messiah. He was a worshipper of the sun god Mithras and remained one even after his so-called conversion to Christianity.

The sun was considered to be "the eye of Mithras." These sun discs can be seen all throughout Christian art and are called "halos." Halos are put above the heads of those Christian characters considered to be divine. This was similar to how sun worshippers ascribed divinity to their gods. In fact, the word "halo" derives from the name "Helios," another prominent sun god.

a noteworthy instance of idolatry

staring at a box
of moving pictures
hooked on a
flat screen fixture
electronic temptations
a combustive mixture

practices of the pagan
day in and day out
what everyone is
talking about

a ritual of
subliminal suggestion
mindless digestion
feeding the flesh
and
polluting the heart

just another part
of every day
where we first
make our way
and stay for hours

abundance of the heart

wounds from a friend
can be trusted
but an enemy
multiplies kisses

near misses
are
no accident

flattery
can turn into battery
stored chemical energy
will always be
converted
real thoughts
will be
asserted

your thought life
becomes a reality
what you feed
is your morality

psych prison

throwing
the mentally ill
into prison
is not the answer
it's a healthcare
disaster

not being able
to resolve it
doesn't absolve
you

it's always
a different story
once your family
is affected

suddenly
they're arrested
when all they wanted
was
therapy

spiritual heresy
gone wrong
but
longsuffering
is a fruit of
The Holy Spirit

only the evil
would
fear it

He hears with
compassion
when the
government fails
to take action

it's never too late

The forerunners of The Messianic Movement, just to name a few:

Todd Bennett - shemayisrael.net
Monte Judah - Lion and Lamb Ministries
Michael Rood - roodawakening
Rabbi Jonathan Cahn - hopeoftheworld.org
Bradford Scott - wildbranch.org

As was his custom, Paul went into the synagogue, and on three Sabbath days he reasoned with them from the scriptures, explaining and proving that the Messiah had to suffer to rise from the dead.

         -     **Acts 17:2**

The symbol of Asclepius is portrayed throughout the medical profession. His symbols are a staff and a snake and are used worldwide as the symbols of medicine. The Greeks knew him as Asklepios and considered him to be a god of healing.

Spirit of Elijah

"And in those days John the Baptist came proclaiming in the wilderness of Judah,
and saying, "Repent, for the reign of the heavens have come near!"
for this is he who was spoken of by the prophet Isaiah, saying, "A voice of one crying in the wilderness, 'Prepare the way of YHWH, make His paths straight. "
– Matthew 3:1-3

John had the spirit of Elijah (Mark 9:11-12) though he did not know it (John 1:21). Yeshua says in Mark 9:11-12, "Elijah indeed, having come first, restores all." And we know that once again; YHWH has declared the end from the beginning, because the spirit of Elijah will once again precede the coming of the Messiah (it already has). Eyes are being opened. Worship is being restored to the way it was before it was corrupted by the Roman Empire. People are beginning to see the plan for the end of the age, and YHWH is speaking to

believers through His Appointed
Times. The spirit of Elijah is
preparing YHWH's people for the
coming of the Kingdom.

*"Remember the Torah of Moses
My servant which I commanded unto
him in Horeb for all Yisrael, with the
statutes and judgments. Behold I will
send you Elijah the prophet before
the coming of the great and dreadful
day of YHWH.*
- Malachi 4:4-5

Yeshua did not create
Christianity. Christianity wouldn't
come about until a couple of
hundred years after Yeshua's death
and resurrection. Emperor
Constantine made it the official
state religion of the Roman Empire
through the Council of Nicaea in
325 C.E.

This confuses some Christians
who did not know that Christianity
was an official religion. Others
believe that Constantine was himself

a Christian but he worshipped Mithra the sun goddess. He had his wife and child murdered after his so-called conversion and he had a mother who used sorcery and divination to locate most, if not all, of the Christian Holy Places. All of this is public knowledge and available to those who study the history of Rome.

Constantine was attempting to salvage a faltering empire. It was clear they could not stop the worship of the Messiah. Despite feeding believers to lions or lighting them as human torches, they got stronger and larger. So he gave the people what they want; only it was mixed with Rome's polytheistic paganism. The Sabbath was outlawed and changed to Sunday (called Rest Day). The Appointed Times were replaced with the pagan holidays: Christmas and Easter. The lunar calendar (Scriptural calendar) was replaced with The Roman Solar Calendar (the names of the days of

the week and months of the years
come from pagan deities).

These are all reasons why
Christians fail to convert Judaism to
the Messiah. Judaism knows the
Messiah will restore Israel, but are
taught by Christians that the
Church has replaced Israel.
Judaism knows that worship was
corrupted by the Roman Empire.
This is why they still use the Lunar
Calendar, observe Sabbath, and
follow the Appointed Times.

When Christians begin telling
them that a Messiah named Yeshua
(not named Yeshua) did away with
the Torah; Christians have now lost
all hope of converting Judaism. Why
would the living Torah tell you not
to obey the Torah? They know there
is a disconnect.

The Spirit of Elijah is restoring
worship back to what Yeshua and
the disciples were doing. This is to

prepare the way for Yeshua and the coming of the kingdom.

The Appointed
Times

Appointed Times, Holy Convocations, Set Apart Rehearsals (Lev 23).

Many people say, they do as the Messiah did, but they do not. The Messiah and the disciples observed Sabbath (Luke 4:16 Mark 6:2 Luke 4:31 Luke 23:56). The Messiah observed the Appointed Times (John 7:2 Luke 22:11 John 2:23-3:21 Zech 14:16). These are only a few of many Scriptures;

Why - if they do as He did - do they not observe Sabbath and The Appointed Times (Lev 23)? The Roman Empire. Of course, the ban on Sabbath and The Appointed Times gets explained in other terms but what it comes down to is: The devil deceived the whole world.

Yeshua fulfilled 4 of the 7 Appointed Times:

1) Passover (He was the Passover sacrifice, the Passover Lamb). Remember, John The Baptist

pronounced Yeshua as the Lamb of Elohim. John was from the line of Aaron; thus he was the only one qualified to make this statement.

2) The Feast of Unleavened Bread - Commemorates the seven day journey of Israel leaving Egypt. They had to eat in haste (unleavened bread).

3) The Feast of First Fruits (When the Barley becomes ripe there is a wave offering of Barley sheaves before YHWH. The seeds of these plants die. Those seeds are then buried under the earth. And then waters (of salvation), waters from the rain germinate those seeds; and new life comes forth from those dead seeds. A new plant then springs up through the earth bearing an abundance of new harvest and new seed. They are commemorating that YHWH had taken those which had died and had been buried; and had now raised it in newness of life. What they are doing is celebrating

the resurrection of life. This is the day that Yeshua came out of the grave. In the Temple, they are all praising YHWH for the resurrection of life, and on this very day Yeshua was resurrected. He fulfilled The Feast of First Fruits.

4) Pentecost. When the Holy Spirit arrived, Pentecost was fulfilled. Pentecost was itself an anniversary of Shavu'ot. On Pentecost, Elohim poured out His Spirit in the Temple on Mount Moriah in Jerusalem, as recorded in Acts 2. The Apostles knew this was the day because they were taught to count the Omer for 50 days (Pente means 50) immediately after the Feast of First Fruits. Thus, they we're all in one accord, in one place.

On Shavu'ot, Elohim appeared in cloud and fire on Mount Sinai and revealed His Torah to the people of Israel. This was the day, Israel said "I do."

The dollar sign ($) used to represent currency is derived from the wand or caduceus carried by the god Mercury (which eventually progressed into a snake wrapped around a pole). The dollar sign was also used by medieval astrologers to denote the planet Mercury. In mythology, Mercury had rule over banking, as well as commercial and financial transactions

Building

Everything which is seen came from what is unseen. It didn't come from nothing. It came from what is unseen. Wisdom was before Genesis 1:1.

Elohim brought me forth as the first of His works, before His deeds of old (Proverb 8:8).

YHWH spoke everything into existence with His Word.

Through faith, through trust, we understand that the worlds were framed by the Word of Elohim. So that the things which are seen were made not of things which do appear. - Hebrew 11:3

Everything in the physical world, originated in the spiritual realm. It is His Word which brings it across that threshold.

By the Word of YHWH the heavens were made, and all their

host by the breath of His mouth. -
Psalm 33:6

Hebrew is the mother tongue. It
is an action language: the seed
language. The seed is the Word of
YHWH (an encapsulated beginning).
His Word made everything seen
which was unseen.

Faith is the substance of things
hoped for, the evidence of things not
seen. - Hebrews 11:1

We must have faith that YHWH's
Word can bring anything He Wills
into existence.

We are not looking on what is
seen, but what is not seen. For what
is seen passes away, but what is not
seen is everlasting. - 2 Corinthians
4:18

There is something about the
written word. Writing brings what is
unseen (or spiritual) into the
physical world. Once the words hit

the paper, they have crossed a threshold. It's almost as if they have gone from one dimension to another. Most importantly, it is YHWH's Word, not ours which has this power.

I noticed a shift once I started writing my prayers down. The prayers we say need to be based on His Word and all of it seems to become eternal once it is written down. There is a movie I recommend watching, called "War Room." The woman of the house begins writing her prayers down along with the Scriptures those prayers are based on. Her prayers get answered. I have noticed this in my own life as well.
YHWH has answered many of my prayers throughout the years. But something I noticed... was that when I started writing them down; my communication with YHWH became even more interesting.

Moses would repeat YHWH's Word back to him.

"And now, I pray, let the power of YHWH be great, as You have spoken, saying, 'YHWH is patient and of great kindness, forgiving wickedness and transgression, but by no means leaving unpunished; visiting the wickedness of the fathers on the children to the third and fourth generation.'
'Please forgive the wickedness of this people, according to the greatness of Your kindness, as You have forgiven this people, from Egypt even until now."
And YHWH said, "I shall forgive, according to your word." - Numbers 14:17-20

YHWH is faithful to His Word. His Word is His Will. Our prayers need to line up with His Word/His Will. Remember that His Word can create, and we are told to build on a rock rather than on sand (Luke 6:47-49).

"Truly, I say to you, whatever you bind on earth shall be bound in heaven, and whatever you loosen on earth shall be loosed in heaven. - Matthew 18:18

When Yeshua rebuked the devil in the wilderness; all three times it was with the Torah. And all three times He said "It is Written."

Again, we see the power of YHWH's Written Word in Daniel 5:5 (The writing is on the wall).

There are some who believe that the original Ten Commandments (the ones Moses broke on the ground) were written on stone that came straight from the throne of YHWH. Moses was away for 40 days, and 40 nights and he did not eat bread or drink water. We know that a person cannot survive under these conditions. It is possible he went through some sort of time warp. Since YHWH is not subject to physical time, Moses could have been translated out of time and into the presence of YHWH (the throne room) where YHWH spoke the Words and gave him the stones with the commandments.

Remember that Mount Zion is located in the heavenly realm, another dimension. This also appears to be the dimension in which the 144,000 are located with the Lamb on the mountain in heaven.

Let us remember that YHWH establishes everything by the mouth of two or three witnesses (Matthew 18:16 - Deuteronomy 17:6 - Deuteronomy 19:15).

Remember that angels serve as witnesses also.

And you, being dead in your trespasses and the uncircumcision of your flesh, He has made alive together with Him, having forgiven you all trespasses, having blotted out the handwriting against us - by the dogmas - which stood against us.

And He has taken it out of the way, having nailed it to the stake. Having stripped the principalities and the authorities, He made a public display of them, having prevailed over them in it. - Colossians 2:13-15

When Yeshua was crucified - He showed not only men, but the entire angelic population - the devil's true colors. Remember that the devil often masquerades as an angel of light.

Angels serve as witnesses to the Written Word of YHWH. By basing your prayers on the Word and writing those prayers down you are establishing them in the eyes of many (unseen) witnesses.

We too, then, having so great a cloud of witnesses all around us, let us lay aside every weight and the sin which so easily entangles us, and let us run with endurance the race put before us. - Hebrews 12:1

demographic

i was
buying all the products
that the rich elite
sold me
buying back the life
that they
stole from me

working for free
a slave
to their psychology
to be who
they have targeted
me to be

every dollar i spend
helps them
put me in prison
their highest good
for me
a sales strategy
selling
self-destruction

Yeshua
is the new us
the rich
don't like that too much

transcending the shadow

exaggerated achievements
a grandiose sense
of self-importance
a little bit
narcissistic
black listed

i must now unfold
the page
how bad
do i want to
change?
that's
that question
that pressuring
makes a man

fragile egos
with
an angry stare
blind spots
unaware

problem sippers
poison mixers
fate missers
lyrics to burn
more of you
to unlearn

examples
to discern
for the
unacceptable
to combat the skeptical

i am a spectacle
of hope
a square
for the eyes
the end
is a
surprise

that defies
common sense
a bit of suspense
you can't put
me in a box
but
it's hard to stop

one thing
life is not
is predictable
improvement is
permissible
souls that are
fixable
saved by the fistful

Eternal Consciousness

What we do translates to eternity. The words we speak, the things we do, the things we write. It is important to speak life; to give a good report. These will be used as evidence of the life we live and the faith we have.

I said in my heart, "Concerning the matter of the sons of men, Elohim examines them, to see if they indeed are beasts." - Ecclesiastes 3:18

Most important are the prayers we have said. Our prayers are the paths we have sown. Remember that YHWH knows every prayer we will ever say. Consider the following Scripture:

And it shall be that before they call, I answer. And while they are still speaking, I hear. - Isaiah 65:24

To understand this Scripture, is to understand the timelessness of prayer and the timelessness of YHWH. After all, if you truly have faith: you should be able to ask for anything - at any time.

Think of the timeline as a kind of time capsule. In the timeline, the things we said, the things we wrote, the things we did; are on display for all eternity and attest to who we are. The things we did and said are a record, a testimony to the life we live and the faith we have.

The Scriptures tell us that predestination comes from foreknowledge (1 Peter 1:1-2). YHWH foreknew who we would be... How we would live.. What we would pray for. Even before the creation of the world, He knew us (1 Peter 1:20). Where in the world we are born, what time in history we are born .. is all based on this predestination which came from His foreknowledge.

Also, a great deal of our lives have to do with promises which YHWH has made to our fathers or promises which they made to Him. A good example would be David and Solomon. Solomon enjoyed a peaceful reign as king .. due to the promises YHWH made to his father David. I would even venture to say that work which our fathers did not complete might get passed on to us, in some cases.

I know that whatever Elohim does is forever. There is no adding to it, and there is no taking from it. Elohim does it, that men should reverence before Him. - Ecclesiastes 3:14

If we are truly eternal creatures, then YHWH knew us from the beginning. He is not affected by time nor is He subject to it. Time is only relative to the earth. A day to YHWH is a thousand years to us.

sixth seal

the bowls
of Yah's wrath
when the smoke
has
darkened
the midday
should take away
any false hope left

no flesh
would stay alive
mushroom clouds
so high

nowhere
to run
from
a 30 million ton
fireball

seeing it all
would be overrated

atheism
cremated

fallout created

the unsealing
of the sixth reason
for those
who believe in
the big bang

renewed testament

the word
"new"
gives the wrong
impression
not the
intention
of the Greek texts

who instead
would
have used "neo"

they used "kainos"
which means
renewed or refreshed
out of respect
the proper
meaning
to be direct

the former
Covenant
is being refreshed
not replaced
when words
are misplaced
they
give the wrong
translation

misguiding
many generations
to believe
something
brand new
replaced the old

what you
were told
is now irrelevant

Vocal Platform
of
the Mind

We know that the mind has a kind of resonating power. We know this because the VOCAL PLATFORM OF THE MIND enables us to pray. The ability to pray in itself is a powerful thing. With our mind we can communicate with our Creator. However, it is also seems to be an open channel for the ENTIRE spiritual realm. The battlefield is in the mind and in the heart. Humans are unique creatures in that we can house spirits (many spirits).
We were given dominion over the earth (Gen 1:26). By resisting and submitting to YHWH, we maintain that dominion.

When we give into the temptations and imaginations of demons, we surrender that control. Without a host, they have no control. And they cannot violate our will.

So then, submit to Elohim. Resist the devil and he shall flee from you. - James 4:7

When we agree with their ideas and imaginations, and act in accordance with such temptations; we have given them the green light. Now they can enter into in our house.

"Or how is one able to enter a strong man's house and plunder his goods, unless he first binds the strong man? And then he shall plunder his house." - Matthew 12:29

They become familiar with us, the more we give in.

A man is slave to whatever has mastered him. - 2 Peter 2:19

Often, many different spirits are working together to get into your house. And we know there is a large number which can enter at one time.

And Yeshua asked him, saying "What is your name?" And he said,

"Legion," because many demons had entered into him. - Luke 8:30

in the fight

rejoice!
His Word is eternal

like silver
tried
in a
furnace of earth

refined
seven times

the battle
is
in the mind
victory over time

nothing
took Him
by surprise
the righteous will rise
to praise the Most High

not even
death
can change
what's next

a cure
for distress

the road signs
say blessed

victory
ahead

it's
not just
the words in red

it's what He did

narrow way

fear and trembling
as the
evening is ending
precede
the blessings
He is sending

praises rising
nothing surprising
YHWH
is in the timing

He is eternal
every day

narrow
is the way
strength
belongs to YHWH

Father of Forever
we were never meant
to be alone
Yeshua has
prepared a home

Selah.

the eyes will be teary
for the worn
and weary

it had to be
this hard
for you to come this far

broken to the core
to live forevermore

to know what it is
to rejoice
at the power
of His voice

Selah.

Works Cited

Resources for Broken Road Ministries:

Yahweh's Evangelical Assembly
PO BOX 31
Atlantic, TX 75551

The House of Yahweh
PO BOX 2498
Abilene, TX 79604

Assemblies of Yahweh
PO BOX C
Bethel, PA 19507

Yahweh's Assembly in Messiah
401 N Roby Farm Rd
Rocheport, MO 65279

Todd Bennett's – Walk in the Light Series- available on
www.shemayisrael.net

Halleluyah Scriptures
PO BOX 2283
Vineland, NJ 08362-2283

Bradford Scott- wildbranch.org

Joel Richardson- The Islamic
Antichrist

Rabbi Jonathan Cahn-
www.hopeoftheworld.org

Michael Rood-
www.rooadawakening.tv

Monte Judah-
www.lionandlambministries.org

Books available by Broken Road Ministries:

Awaken the Dawn
Jesus Set Me Free
Master of the Worlds
Lost Sheep
Resist the Devil
Rise
War in Heaven
Battle-axe
The Messianic Movement
The Watchers

For a free copy of any of these books, write to:

Broken Road Ministries
P.O. Box 780751
Orlando, FL 32878

Specify which book you are interested in receiving.

Made in the USA
Columbia, SC
05 October 2022

68629747R00115